# The Career Positioning Challenge: Essential Career Perspectives and Insights

Dr. David P. Peltz

Foreword by
Dr. John H. Wilson

## Disclaimer

The information provided within this book is for general informational purposes only. While we try to keep the information up-to-date and correct, there are no representations or warranties, express or implied, about the completeness, accuracy, reliability, suitability or availability with respect to the information, products, services, or related graphics contained in this eBook for any purpose. Any use of this information is at your own risk. If you wish to apply ideas contained in this book, you are taking full responsibility for your actions.

The methods describe within this book are the author's personal thoughts. They are not intended to be a definitive set of instructions for this project. You may discover there are other methods and materials to accomplish the same end result.

The author has made every effort to ensure the accuracy of the information within this book was correct at time of publication. The author does not assume and hereby disclaims any liability to any party for any loss, damage, or disruption caused by errors or omissions, whether such errors or omissions result from accident, negligence, or any other cause.

ISBN: 9781973836339

# Dedication

To everyone who wants to take the next step in their careers towards achieving their professional goals and aspirations – may you find value in these pages.

# Contents

# Foreword

## Dr. John H. Wilson, Ph.D.

If you were being honored at the end of your career and a close colleague and friend of many years got up to give the toast, how would you want them to describe your life's work? A career could very easily be characterized as a life story framed in a professional context, much like this kind of retirement tribute. No matter whether you work for the same organization for your entire professional life, change jobs frequently, or primarily pursued entrepreneurial endeavors, it is likely that the story would depict countless examples of adaptation.

What is adaptation, exactly, when it comes to your career journey? It is more than just changing a routine, but somehow stops short of complete transformation (though there are appropriate times for both of these as well). Adaptation draws on current strengths, capabilities, and experiences, yet also adds to them or applies them to new circumstances. Adaptation also involves pulling back from activities that no longer have relevance and focusing on others that have more impact due to new circumstances.

Some might argue that adaptation wasn't important in their career since they worked for the same company doing the same job for decades. Perhaps that was the case for some in the past, but the emerging state of exponential technologies, economic transformation, and social change is creating a turbulent, continuously-changing work environment. In such an environment, even staying in the same place requires assertive and intentional adaptation. This involves continuous learning, self-reflection, and the flexibility to shift in response to new paradigms, disruptive alternatives to the status quo, and increasing competitive pressures in virtually every industry.

Change is often uncomfortable, so the idea of adaptation may cause some apprehension. However, taking initiative to regularly advance core job skills or to expand competencies to learn supplemental disciplines is akin to buying options for future changes that can't be predicted with certainty. If you enjoy your current work, and the need for your services in this area persists, such new skills strengthen your ability to be effective. Likewise, if your interest level or market demand begins to wane, new capabilities create new opportunities that provide the flexibility to adapt to the changing environment.

As you ponder the first question above about what you would want to be said about your career accomplishments, here are a few suggestions:

- Dream big – it is your life's work, so consider the endless possibilities and ignore any obstacles that might impede your success
- Focus on more on what you want to accomplish and less on the exact progression of jobs/roles
- Assume that you have the ability to succeed at everything you attempt

- Set aside financial practicality – of course you must address your financial obligations along the way, but for the purposes of this idealized reality you are creating for yourself, assume that this all works out align the way
- Have fun considering all the possibilities for your remarkable career

This career story will allow you to begin with the end in mind – no matter where you are in your journey. Whether you are five years away from your retirement toast or 40 years, you can dream big and embrace endless possibilities. Therefore, your career position represents where you are at this moment in relation to your vision to have more clarity about how to invest your time, energy and resources. Is it the right time to start a new degree program? How about a professional certificate? Or, are there big changes in your area of expertise that warrant intentional reading and research to stay ahead of the curve in your field? An established career position helps to keep questions, like these, at top of your mind while providing insight into the best answers in response to changes or disruption in your professional environment.

Getting from today to your retirement toast is where you have the most work to do since there are immediate factors to account for such as paying your bills, getting or keeping a job, and balancing all other facets of your life to ensure that you can enjoy the journey. This is where The Career Transition Challenge can help you to clarify actions you can take right now that can help you to achieve the vison you have for your career.

In his first book, The Military Transition Challenge, Dr. Peltz provided a useful framework and practical steps to address immediate needs and circumstances while advancing the longer-term goals when transitioning from the military to civilian life. Many of these ideas are equally applicable for others who are facing career transition between jobs, industries, or areas of focus. So, in this, his second volume, The Career Positioning Challenge, he has expanded these ideas for individuals who aspire to have a meaningful career that they can look back upon with pride and satisfaction.

This practical guide will not only help with an immediate transition, but will also offer insight into how to develop a mindset of continuous adaptation, while taking meaningful steps to pursue learning and experiences that give you the flexibility to sense and respond to opportunities and challenges that come your way. Cheers to you!

Dr. John H. Wilson, Ph.D.
Author, motivational speaker, & founder of Strategic Collisions International

# Preface

READ THIS FIRST: The Way this Book is Written

Please read the sections and chapters in the order presented. Each section builds upon the previous section to create layers of knowledge and insight. Think of it in terms of building a house. While we may want to have the roof built to shade us from the elements, we need to have a solid foundation and supporting walls first.

I recently published my first book on career positioning entitled *The Military Transition Challenge: Essential Perspectives for Civilian Career Positioning.* While it was primarily focused towards military and veterans, I received many requests from non-military regarding content applications that were directly applicable to contemporary workplace environments. This current book was intended to be an extension and companion text to the first, and it does just that – bringing career positioning into a generalized working professional perspective. It focuses on the cognitive awareness surrounding critical guiding elements involving career positioning. It also offers details of personal and professional insights and accounts about what career positioning is, the different types career positioning, and impacts of effective career positioning. It concludes with applications about career positioning considerations.

As discussed in my previous book, my life has not necessarily been filled with glamour and fame. Rather, quite the opposite is true. I have overcome many personal and professional challenges throughout my career. On a personal level, I have come from a family of divorce, persevered through abusive step parents and bullies, and overcome poor grades in high school. On a professional level, I have endured the frustrations of transitioning from the military to civilian way of life on three different occasions and have worked in half a dozen different career sectors. A few of the outcomes from these experiences include understanding how to position myself for promotions and advancement, learning how to expand and broaden my business acumen, and how to prepare myself for future opportunities to lead others. These lessons have contributed greatly to my development in ways that have enhanced my career positioning. My hope is that they will prove valuable to you as well.

I have learned from each career transition and subsequent career positioning. I can break down my 30-year career in the following overlapping categories: military and civilian law enforcement, corporate and defense contracting, higher education and consulting. These categories overlap in many ways. I am not one to sit still, I have always felt the need to keep pushing, and doing, and accomplishing more; and always having a back-up plan to my back-up plan.

## *Military and Civilian Law Enforcement*

The first six years of my military career I spent equal parts overseas in Europe and stateside mastering my security police craft. I separated from the military and went to work for state corrections. While working state corrections, I joined the U.S. Air Force Reserves Security Forces. I resigned from the reserves after two and a half years, and later resigned from state corrections after five and a half years of service. I then started working at the Air National Guard as a Security Forces supervisor. Three years later I was discharged from the military under medical conditions; and that began the second phase in my career. My dedication to excelling in my profession led to more opportunities. The results of my efforts led to several awards, recognitions, and promotions, thereby increasing my future positioning opportunities.

## *Corporate and Defense Contracting*

During this phase, I had been periodically working as a part time business consultant (mostly pro bono) when an opportunity arose. I worked in retail management for about a year, then took a job as a college recruiter for about a year and a half. While the pay was less as a college recruiter than that of a retail manager, I was working fewer hours: retail was about 70-80 hours a week, college recruiting was 40 hours a week. I then accepted a job working as a temporary contractor for a few months for a defense contractor before being hired on full time. I worked for the defense contractor for the next nine years in various positions. I started off in property management as a contractor then moved to finance in a full-time capacity. I also worked operations policies and procedures, engineering property management support, program manager certification, and was a classified engineering lab manager. I then was offered, and accepted, a job as a program manager in the information technology sector; it paid nearly double my defense salary. After about a year in the technology sector, I was laid off. This led to the third phase in my career. My determination and flexibility opened doors to many internal opportunities. Some of these opportunities broadened my business acumen, while others provided networking leads that proved useful during company reorganization periods.

## *Higher Education and Consulting*

During my third year working for the defense contractor, I formalized my part time business and leadership consulting business. During my seventh year at the defense contractor, I started teaching college courses part time. When I was laid off from the technology sector, consulting and teaching became my central areas of focus.

## *Summary*

All told, I have worked in six different industry sectors and have held over two dozen professional titles. Several have been due to promotions, many have been because of internal/external lateral moves, a few have been the result of layoffs or organizational restructuring. Virtually all the positions I have held involved deliberate career positioning.

Not all my transitions were easy, in fact, most were not. They did become "easier" as I began to realize some of the common and critical elements within the career positioning process. Once I started accepting these elements, and their underlying elemental patterns, I created a plan and successfully navigated the career positioning environment.

I have achieved a level of mastery in career positioning not for the number of jobs I have held (there have been a few) but rather because how I have learned, navigated, and mastered career positioning opportunities over time. I do not claim to know everything, but I do know what I know; and, perhaps more importantly, I have come to know what I do not know. One of my personal mantras is that I am a "Jack of many trades, and master of some". Perhaps the greatest take-aways from my career track have been: always have a large achievable goal, and always maintain a positive optimistic outlook about my future. These two critical attitudinal foci have enabled me to keep the momentum going and overcome many challenging obstacles.

This book is intended to provide guidance and clarity while offering effective approaches to career positioning. Whether you are:

- wanting to promote within your organization or outside your company;
- looking for a lateral move internally or externally for better career alignment;
- have been affected by a reduction in force/reorganization;
- wanting to remain competitive in your career/industry;
- wanting to retire;
- wanting to change careers or industries;

- or are simply wanting a change…

then this book is for you. Take charge of your career and make your professional future your reality.

# Acknowledgements

Thank you to my wife, Julie, and son, David, for their constant love and support. Because of them, I am always striving to achieve more.

Thank you to all my professors, peers, colleagues, managers, and leaders who have had a positive impact on my education and career.

Thank you to the best military supervisors throughout my military service: Rocky Grider, Jerry Turley, Dr. Dana Biddulph, and Connie Brannock. Your leadership and guidance was instrumental to my professional development – this book is for you!

# Operational Definitions

Career Positioning

career
1. a. A chosen pursuit; a profession or occupation.
1. b. The general course or progression of one's working life or one's professional achievements: an officer with a distinguished career; a teacher in the midst of a long career.
(American Heritage® Dictionary of the English Language, Fifth Edition)

position
1. A place or location.
2. A strategic area occupied by members of a force.
4. An advantageous place or location.
5. A situation as it relates to the surrounding circumstances.
6. A point of view or attitude on a certain question.
(American Heritage® Dictionary of the English Language, Fifth Edition)

career positioning
1. The conscious choice to strategically plan, proactively prepare, and incrementally complete decisive actions towards achieving a career goal.
– David P. Peltz, Ph.D., 2017

# Part I: Guiding Career Positioning Elements

1. First Step
2. Critical Reflection
3. Motivation
> Extrinsic motivation
> Intrinsic motivation
4. Locus of Control
> External locus of control
> Internal locus of control
5. Stress Versus Frustration
6. Conscious Choice

# 1 - First Step

All our greatest journeys and accomplishments start with taking a first step. In some cases, that first step is actually a huge leap. If I had not taken that first terrifying and fearful step in 1999, I would not have completed my college education. Not only did I succeed in this leap, it catapulted my ambition and dreams to ultimately achieve a doctor of philosophy. Your dreams can be realized. You just need to take that first step...even if it sometimes looks like you will be stepping off a cliff.

You may be asking yourself, what is so terrifying about attending college? My simple answer is we all have fears of some sort. They may not be scary monsters or dark alleys or lions and bears, but we all have fears...it is natural. Many times, these fears are bourn from internalized experiences or events from our past, or perhaps even originating from a compartmentalized or long-forgotten childhood event. For me, my fear of failing in school was based on having two abusive step parents. Both had ensured, through physical and emotional abuse, that my childhood self-confidence was shattered. They also made it overwhelming clear, that I was unintelligent and would never amount to anything. This constant brainwashing over several years was reflected in my poor grades from elementary through high school. That being said, I did perform very well in art classes, and scored well in all categories of the Armed Services Vocational Aptitude Battery (ASVAB), with most scores being in the low to upper 80s. When I entered the military right after high school, I did have concerns surrounding my intellectual capability. I did well in my military training with most of my scores being in the mid 80s on average, which boosted my self-confidence.

When I was almost 30 years old, I took my first two college courses at the somewhat incessant aggressive urging of one of my fellow Security Forces colleagues and supervisor (thank you D.B.) – he was working on his master's degree at the time. I was terrified, I still did not think I was smart enough, and I did not want to fail. Failure would have just reinforced what had been imposed upon me in my childhood. I passed both courses with As. A short time later I enrolled into a full-time bachelor's degree program. During my undergraduate program, I realized I was smart. Which is to say I had much more aptitude and potential than I previously realized. I graduated with an A average. I then decided to roll right into my master's program, and again graduated with an A average. Despite enduring challenging personal relationships during this period in my life, I received A averages in both degrees. It was also during my master's program that I set the goal to get a doctorate degree someday.

When I talk to people who are debating the issue of attending college, I tell everyone the same thing: starting college is like having children or getting a puppy…there is never a great time to start, it is just something you commit to doing and you do it. And, just like raising children or a puppy, you learn much of what you need to know along the way and from listening to others' experiences who have children and dogs. There are many more personal and professional layers to this story, the important thing here is to take note that I had overcome a huge fear of failure by directly confronting it head on.

Maybe your first step is also deciding to attend college. Maybe it is about changing careers or jobs or industry or work location. Maybe you are wanting to take the next step to advance your career but are not sure where to start. Maybe you know where to start but are afraid of failing or falling short. Break the cycle of indecision, doubt, and procrastination…the ONLY thing stopping you from taking that first step is you. I urge you to just stop for a few moments and take some deep breaths, relax…and just breathe. Now, take that first step.

# 2 - Critical Reflection

In adult learning theory, there is a principle known as critical reflection or critical self-reflection (Mezirow, 1991; Mezirow, & Taylor, 2009). The theory states, adults learn from doing followed by a period of reflection about the experience they just had. This solidifies the knowledge and lessons gained from that experience. When I reflected on my experiences, patterns began to emerge about the things that worked well and those that did not work so well. I then repeated and improved upon those things that worked well, and learned from what did not work well in an effort to avoid making the same mistakes again. Much like riding a bike, learning to drive, or learning to swim, we can reflect on our careers to identify various patterns that are likely to set us up for success.

For example, when I began reflecting on what was working well for me in college, I found that when I started my assignments earlier, the better my grades were. Similarly, when interviewing for jobs, I found preparation to be paramount. I researched the company I was interviewing for, I had prepared questions for the interviewers, I gave myself extra time to get to the interview on time, I had prepared answers in advance for anticipated interview questions, and I practiced interviewing with trusted colleagues. When I was seeking an internal position to move into, I did all the above PLUS getting to know the hiring manager and their staff prior to the interview(s). All these activities were based upon reflecting on past experiences on what worked well and what did not. Some of the things I listed may see like common sense…and some are. The key is that they were all deliberate conscious choices to improve my position towards achieving a goal.

Consider the example of allowing extra time to get to an interview. We all know we should show up on time for an interview (at least if you want a shot at the job). Being prior military, I totally get the whole "show up to work on time" thing. In the military, we were taught to always be 15 minutes early for every appointment. One of our military sayings is "early is on time; on time is late." So why am I so focused on the "extra" time facet. I have prepared for interviews in the past and planned to arrive 15 minutes early. However, on a few occasions, I encountered unexpected traffic, or was delayed due to a traffic accident or a long slow train, or had car trouble, or had difficulty finding parking, or had difficulty finding the office or building where the interview was being held. All these things either caused me to be "on time" or a little late for the interview. I am not claiming these things prevented me from getting the job, but they did make me sweat more and created some anxiety about not arriving earlier for the interview.

Another example to consider: getting to know the hiring manager and their staff prior to the interview. This became a factor when I overheard I was passed up for a position because the hiring manager and their team did not know who I was or anything about me or my job performance. They were impressed with my qualifications, but they did not know me. They opted to hire someone the team members had recommended, who was slightly less qualified than me. That decision was not wrong or illegal. It simply demonstrated that having a strong network would increase my odds for getting hired into a position.

After learning from those experiences, I made a deliberate effort to get to know potential hiring managers and their teams. I once found myself in an awkward situation soon after I was promoted into a position. A few months after receiving the promotion, I was informed that they were dissolving my job due to budgetary constraints, and I was given 30 days (not a lot of time) to find another position within the company. I started talking to managers and team members in my workplace network who I had worked with (but not for) in the recent past. It paid off! I approached one of the managers letting him know I was available. He jumped at the opportunity to have me join his team. Within three weeks I was working for him directly. I am pretty sure this set a human resource record for efficient hiring practice, showing it did not take two to three months to properly hire someone into a job. Had I not taken the time to get to know the manager and his team members prior to the dissolution of my position, I am very confident this opportunity would not have materialized.

As adults, we learn from our experiences. Critical reflection ensures those lessons learned are locked into our conscious memory. I am constantly reflecting on the experiences I have. I take notes, I ask questions to others, I discuss my experiences with others; all in an effort to lock down those patterns and lessons in my mind. Just like knowing what time to leave for work each day, each event and experience serve as data points for me to reflect on how to create a better plan and better position my career.

# 3 - Motivation

Motivation is an interesting and intriguing topic. To note, there is a distinction between motivation and inspiration. One definition of inspiration stated it is an "excitement of the mind or emotions" (Inspiration, 2016), and another definition stated it is a "stimulation or arousal of the mind" (Inspiration, 2014). Whereas motivation is behaviorally based in actions producing positive or negative consequences (Bandura, 1969). Furthermore, motivation can be subdivided into intrinsic and extrinsic motivations.

## *Extrinsic Motivation*

Extrinsic motivation states people do things to avoid a particular result or achieve a specific reward. It can almost be viewed as a sort of quid pro quo; if this, then that. Extrinsic motivators can come in the forms of punishment avoidance. For example: if you habitually show up for work late, you may receive a reprimand or be fired. It can also be in the form of tangible rewards. For example: money, recognition, promotion, prestige, a physical object, power, etc. Another example may be if you complete a college education, your career prospects may provide for greater income potential (Vroom, 1964).

I was extrinsically motivated to get a bachelor's degree. When I started going to college full time, I viewed it as my ticket to a better life and greater financial reward for my work. I was motivated by the monetary benefit that came with the degree. I was also motivated by the achievement aspect because not many of my friends and immediate family had a college education at the time. I was driven by the fact that if I did not complete a college education, I was more than likely destined to work in a less than desirable position within a company. I was motivated to be a positive role model for my son, and others in my sphere of influence. These were also the driving forces behind me completing my master's degree and Ph.D.

### *Intrinsic Motivation*

Intrinsic motivation states people do things because they like or love doing them. For example, helping others in need, going to college (i.e. life-long learning), engaging in sport and leisure activities, various hobbies, listening to music, mentoring and coaching, reading, learning new things, traveling, etc. The positive outcome is the joy of doing or participating in these activities (Deci, 1975; Deci, & Ryan, 1985; Deci, & Ryan, 2002).

I was intrinsically motivated to complete a doctorate degree. Early on in my master's program, I told my classmates I was going to complete a doctorate.

By that time, I had dismissed the false belief that I was not smart, and I had fallen in love with learning in a formal academic setting. Admittedly, there was a bit of an extrinsic factor because of the inherent prestige of being a doctor (not a physician), but still, the drive was from deep within me. Not only did I love learning for the joy of it, I wanted others to know I loved learning too. So much so, that I was driven to complete a terminal degree. An achievement that only about 4% of the U.S. population has accomplished. I was also internally driven by being the best fatherly role model to my son. I wanted my son to grow up knowing he too could achieve anything he wanted in life.

In some cases, the underlying factors that motivate us can have a sort of duality. As noted above, my desire to be a good role model for my son and going to college. Both had aspects of extrinsic motivation (i.e., the notoriety) and intrinsic motivation (i.e., for the love and enjoyment of doing them). Understanding where our motivation originates helps us to understand what is driving our perceptions of control and our decision making. The source of motivation can be internally driven for the joy of doing or pursuing something or it can externally driven by positive or negative possibilities. Being self-aware about what drives us to do or pursue certain things is typically sourced through critical reflection. Knowing what you want to do or accomplish or achieve, are goals; understanding what is driving you towards those goals, is motivation. Possessing motivational self-awareness will influence the choices you make towards achieving solid career positioning.

# 4 - Locus of Control

Locus of control centers around one's perception towards the type and degree of influence a person has over their environment. Phares and Lamiell (1975) stated "I-E [internal-external locus of control] deals with the extent to which individuals attribute the responsibility for the occurrence of reinforcement to themselves (internals) or to forces outside themselves (externals)" (p. 23). Understanding the two types of locus of control will help us determine what things we have control and influence over, and which we do not.

## *External Locus of Control*

Boone, de Brabander, and van Witteloostuijn (1996) stated:

> Those with an external locus of control see themselves as relatively passive agents and believe that the events in their lives are due to uncontrollable forces. Externals feel that the things they want to achieve are dependent on luck, chance and powerful persons or

institutions. They believe that the probability of being able to control their lives by their own actions and efforts is low. (p. 668)

Things we surely do not have control over are perhaps things like the weather, other people's actions, and the price of fuel. That being said, it could be argued that in fact we do have control over aspects and elements of each of these items. For example, we do have control over how we react to the weather, how we can potentially influence others, and which gas station we choose to purchase gasoline from.

## *Internal Locus of Control*

Boone et al. (1996) stated:

Conversely, those with an internal locus of control see themselves as active agents, feel that they are masters of their fates and trust in their capacity to influence the environment. Internals assume that they can control the events in their lives by effort and skill. (p. 668)

Things we surely do have control over are things like our own actions and responses, our conscious decisions towards our career plans, and our interactions and influences over other people. Here again, it could be argued, that we are never fully in control of each of these things. For example, some of our actions and responses may be involuntary in a hostile situation (fight or flight response), or that there are obstacles preventing us from achieving our career plans, or that other people will make their own decisions regardless of our level of influence over them.

The key to understanding the differences between external and internal locus of control does NOT lie in the potential opposing arguments but rather in the definitions themselves. Ultimately, we choose (consciously or subconsciously) what type of environmental control we have in a situation. It is up to us as individuals to determine which type of control we will possess and own it. To be more successful at career positioning, must make the conscious choice to exhibit internal locus of control.

I can recall, taking control of my environment on several occasions. As a young airman in the U.S. Air Force, I was just experiencing life and work as it came at me. I was having fun, doing my job, and just living. Early on, I made several poor decisions, which led to less than desirable professional situations that had a negative impact on my career. No show stoppers, but definitely things to give me a wake-up call. At that time in my life, I tended blame others for my misfortunes rather than look to myself about what I could have done differently. So, I made a conscious shift in my perspective. I took control of my life and began holding myself accountable for my career. I started working with my supervisor who helped me get on track (thank you R.G.).

When I went to my second military base, I expanded on this new pattern of taking control of my career. As a newly promoted supervisor, I was given the "problem children" to supervise – I exceeded in turning them around and getting them on the right career path. I then set my sights on not only doing a good job but wanting to do a *great* job. I studied and memorized everything I could about my day-to-day job as a Security Forces member. This extra effort paid off again (thank you J.T.), and I received an extremely rare recognition for my job excellence – U.S. Air Force Outstanding Performer. After that, I was hooked on taking charge of my career and being an over-achiever. Every job I had after that point, I always ensured I left my mark by doing something cool that improved the environment I was working in. Another example I recall was when I worked at a defense contractor as a contracted employee. I received a one-year renewable contract as a property analyst. The ramp up was a slow on-the-job-training process that took about 12 to 16 weeks to complete. At the end of my three months I handed my supervisor an 80-page training guide I had created based upon my notes, observations, and experience. The training book reduced the original 12-16 weeks down to only two weeks. Shortly thereafter I was brought on as a permanent full-time employee. The training guide was still being used nine years later when I left the company.

Taking control of your career can be fun and rewarding. It is also full of challenges. Challenges that can be overcome through experiential observation and critical reflection. Challenges that can more easily be overcome when applying lessons learned from yourself and others.

Unfortunately, many people live their professional lives waiting for something good to happen (external locus of control). I usher a challenge for you to take control of your career and make those opportunities your reality (internal locus of control). The adage of Success = Preparation + Opportunity (Bobby Unser; Zig Ziglar; Jimmy Johnson) is a mantra for those persons who have taken control of their careers. Make your career become the career you want it to be.

# 5 - Stress Versus Frustration

I have found there is a distinction and notable difference between stress and frustration. It has been my experience that stress tends to be a cognitive subconscious response to a situation or event. Conversely, I have observed in myself (and others) that frustration was an emotionally based response. While the two may appear similar, they are addressed differently. To help differentiate between stress and frustration, career types that encounter stressful situations consist of law enforcement, first responders, fire fighters, medial/emergency personnel, and military members. Jobs and careers that have an inherent risk to life (yours and/or others) evoke stress. Frustration is an emotional response derived from experiencing less than desirable situations or results – what may frustrate you may not create frustration for me or someone else. For example, experiencing a major printer jam and a subsequent paper cut while trying to make 100 copies of the latest sales report that will be presented to leadership in five minutes is NOT stressful – there is NO risk to life. It is however, frustrating because the printer is jammed, you are on a short timeline, your job may or may not be at risk (a whole other issue to be dealt with), and now you must find a bandage for your paper cut – all are less than desirable situations and results but definitely NOT potentially deadly or physically harmful (except for maybe the paper cut).

In the military, law enforcement, and similar lines of work, we are taught that remaining calm counteracts stress. Remaining calm in stressful situations can seem to slow time and enhance your senses. I have been in stressful situations in my career. By remaining calm we put ourselves in a state of mind to focus on the situation rather than the emotion.

I recall a time when I was in the military on my way to work. It was mid-morning, I was in uniform and was driving down a main road (a 45-mph zone) not too far from my house. I noticed about six or seven cars had pulled off the side of the road and everyone was on their cell phones. I soon figured out why. About 50 yards up the road a late model pick-up truck had struck an electrical pole head on. The nearest person was 20 yards from the accident. I quickly parked my truck on the opposite side of the street, and ran over to the truck. There was a young woman in her early twenties on the driver's side of the vehicle. The windshield was smashed just above the steering wheel. The woman was bleeding from wounds on her face and head. I introduced myself, and started talking to her in a calm manner. I asked her a few questions and did a quick injury assessment. She had indicated she had not been wearing her seatbelt. I quickly determined she had facial injuries and more than likely had broken both her legs and an arm. I remained calm and took basic first aid measures to address the bleeding. Emergency medical personnel arrived in less than 10 minutes, wrote down my contact information, and took over the scene. By the time first responders arrived, the car count on the side of the road was well over a dozen vehicles, yet I was the only person helping the victim. One of the emergency personnel called me later and thanked me for my help and told me had I not tended to the accident victim, there was a very high probability she would have gone into shock, or perhaps worse. The good news is, she survived.

Years later, my son, who was also in the military at the time, did the exact same thing for a man he witnessed in a motorcycle accident. The young man did not have a helmet on and had severe head and facial injuries. My son, too, remained calm and tended to the accident victim until first responders arrived. The man survived.

Possessing the correct perspective about what is stressful versus what is frustrating is critical. I have been in many frustrating positions in the work place. For example, one time I joined a meeting with my supervisor and a couple team members to provide a status update for a major project. I arrived early and got set up. My supervisor arrived and told me the other two members got pulled into another meeting at the last moment. He stated it would just be the two of us, and another person he wanted in on the update. I started presenting the project status and after about 10 minutes he had me stop. He said the other person present was actually from human resources and was not there for the project update but for another reason. Then they informed me my position had been dissolved due to budgetary reductions as a part of a departmental reorganization. Yes, that was how I was notified about the department reduction. Admittedly, I was taken aback – this was not the meeting I had planned for. I was not stressed however; very frustrated – most definitely. Again, I remained calm.

Why was I not stressed? Because no one's life was in danger. However, I was very frustrated by the delayed notification tactics, and for being blind-sided in a meeting that had a very different agenda. I was also frustrated because I knew I had a lot of work ahead of me to secure another position in the company and only had a short period of time to overcome this challenge. And I did, in record time, because I had been positioning my career properly. Now if you were to tell me a pride of hungry lions was on the loose in the building while I was being told this news…that would have been stressful!

I challenge you to acknowledge the difference between stress and frustration. I challenge you to be consciously aware the next time you encounter a stressful or frustrating situation. I challenge you consciously differentiate between the two reactions so that you respond accordingly. A slight shift in perspective between these two things will increase your level of awareness and help you properly address the situation.

# 6 - Conscious Choice

This is another of my favorite topics. Early in my career, I began making a series of conscious choices. The more I reflected on my choices the more I began to realize there were times in my life when I was just making decisions, and other times when I was making conscious choices. When I reflected even more, I came to the realization that the more conscious choices I made, the more focused and self-aware I became, and the more positive outcomes resulted from my choices. About mid-way through my career, it was brought to my attention that I should incorporate more conscious choice into my personal life as well. When I did, better things started happening there too, and a short time later I met my wife, Julie.

Conscious choice provides a grounding baseline of sorts. When conscious choice is applied, amazing things start to happen. You become engaged, empowered, and aware of what is happening around you and why. After working in a job or career for a while, we become comfortable with our routine. We make decisions and answer questions as easy as eating and drinking. Have you ever decided to do something (like say, attend a meeting), then totally forgot to attend the meeting? Hopefully it was not an important meeting because that would create a potentially frustrating situation (reflect on previous section on Stress Versus Frustration). The reason this occurs is because we are not making conscious choices…we are just deciding. Conscious choice pairs nicely with internal locus of control when you make a conscious choice to take control of your career.

Generally speaking, I like to think of myself as a fun easy-going guy. I do not actively go around trying to make people and employees miserable – however, I have met managers who seem to pride themselves on this tactic. Rather, I try to ensure everyone has a positive outlook and that their day goes well. That is my conscious choice. I have also made the conscious choice to always have a backup plan for my career. That back up plan has taken many forms over the years depending on where I was in my career and what the job environment was like at the time.

For example, when I was in the military for the third time, I made the conscious choice to start attending college. This was a goal, but it was also a backup plan. My plan A was to retire from the military – finally. I say finally because it had taken me several years to position myself into a full-time job with the Air National Guard. I had been back in the military for about a year and a half, and it was five months after 9/11/2001. I recall I was working a crazy schedule of 12-hour shifts that were actually closer to 15-hour shifts. We had to arm up with our weapons, then drive out to our posts; and vice versa after our shift was over. It was early February 2002, and we had just had a bad rain storm come through. The rain and winds knocked over 30 feet of shared fencing between my and my neighbor's house. Being the fit military guy, I repaired the fencing. As I finished up and was climbing down from a section of the fence, the fence gave way tossing me about 10 feet. I remember hearing a loud "crack" sound, and thought to myself "oh, that cannot be good". Nope. I had crushed my right ankle, and fractured and shifted both my tibia and fibula out of alignment. A couple of surgeries and a year and a half later, I was medically discharged from military service. My back up plan (completing a college degree) was now my plan A. Fortunately, I completed my bachelor's degree the same month I was discharged from the military, and within a few weeks I had secured a job.

Continuing with conscious choice, the first job I had after the military was as a retail manager. I liked the job, but the hours were crazy long. Anyone who has worked retail management will attest it is very fast paced, and it is typical to work 60 to 70 hours a week. I worked as a hardlines (all merchandise except clothing) assistant store manager and was responsible for 75% of the overall store merchandise and about 50% of the daily operations. There were six other assistant store managers who worked there, one each in: human resources, security, front end customer service, logistics, soft-lines (only clothing), and a second much smaller hardlines department. Originally, I started with three full-time employees and eight part-time employees. About eight months into my job the store manager shifted the work assignments and I was left with one full-time employee and two part-time employees. I sensed something was amiss since the employees I used to have working for me were shifted over to the other smaller departments. This left my department significantly understaffed and the other departments significantly overstaffed. When I met with the store manager about this staffing issue I was told to "deal with it". At the time, I was working on my master's degree and had several contacts at the university I was attending. I made the conscious choice to position myself to make a move to work for the university. Several weeks later when the work situation at the retail store reached a tipping point, I made the conscious choice to part from my retail management job and started a job working for the university the following week.

Another conscious choice that enabled me to capitalize on career positioning was when I was working for a defense contractor. I had been working at the defense contractor for eight and a half years and had completed my doctorate one year before. I noticed there was not much opportunity for me to advance at the company, so I began applying for jobs outside the company. I had a couple of interviews and one company looked very promising. It was working in the technology software sector as a program manager. They offered me the job and it came with a 60% pay increase. I was faced with a tough decision: stay with a company that I had nine years of tenure and experience or take a new job with a large salary and responsibility increase. I made the conscious choice to capitalize on my career positioning and went with the latter.

A cool thing happens when you make a conscious choice to position your career: new opportunities start presenting themselves. Sometimes they are exactly what you are looking for. Sometimes they happen at just the right moment. Sometimes they happen when you least expect them to in an area you had not previously considered, and you are in a position to capitalize on the opportunity.

# Part II: Career Positioning Explained

# 7 - What is Career Positioning

"Career positioning is the conscious choice to strategically plan, proactively prepare, and incrementally complete decisive actions towards achieving a career goal." – David P. Peltz, Ph.D., 2017

While related to career transitioning, career positioning is quite different. Transitioning is reactive by nature. When we think about transitioning we think about going from one place or state of being to another place or state of being. Transitioning evokes a starting point and an ending point. Transitioning is about taking that journey from point A to point B. Transitioning is about reacting to a present state or situation.

Career positioning is about being proactive. It is about ensuring we are already in a state or place to take advantage of an opportunity. It is about making sure we are ready BEFORE a situation or opportunity presents itself. Career positioning is about preparing ourselves with all the necessary skills, experience, education, and network needed to achieve our desired career state well in advance of achieving our goal.

## _Significance of Career Positioning_

The significance of career positioning resides in the preparation. The more time you have to prepare, the more you can apply a concentrated effort towards being prepared. In other words, the more time you have to prepare, the less frustration you will experience during the preparation. Creating that time allows us the luxury of forethought. Career positioning then allows for proper planning and execution of those plans. We can think about it in simpler terms of washing a car. If we rush through washing our car by hand, we will inevitably miss some dirt on the outside and there will be water spots on the body and windows because we were rushing to dry it. We may not even have time to wax the outside or to vacuum the inside. However, if we start earlier and have a bit more time to build our plan, we can wash, dry, wax, and vacuum our car and it will look great. There are those of you who are thinking "Why wash your car when you can take it through a car wash?" I will answer that question with a question: would you leave your career in someone else's hands? I think we all know how that would work out. I shamefully admit, on occasion, I have taken my car through the car wash. They are not proud moments. When all is said and done, while the vehicle looks better than before the wash, there are still spots that were missed. Sometimes, I even use the car wash just to get the car to a state where I can handle washing it myself – sometimes I just need a little help. So, my point here is, while you can definitely have help with your career positioning, you should take pride and ownership, and take an active role in your career positioning. Solid planning and preparation will prevent a frustrating reactionary rush job from happening. Remember career positioning is a about being proactive towards achieving your career goals for the long term, not just getting a job.

# 8 - Career Positioning Transparency

You may be asking yourselves what does transparency have to do with career positioning? Simply stated, there is a need for transparency with ourselves, and how we approach our career positioning. Transparency, in terms of self-awareness, transparency in terms of self-honesty, and transparency in terms of planning. These levels of transparency play a vital role later when we discuss Experiential Extraction. For now, though, we need to understand each of these levels of transparency.

## *Self-Awareness Transparency*

This is progression that follows after critical reflection. When we critically reflect, we become more aware about ourselves, our experiences, and our personal and professional paths. Self-awareness transparency involves capturing key learning from experiential lessons. It causes us to dig deep into our reflection to become critically aware about not only the large or impactful events, decisions, and experiences but also the small seemingly insignificant ones too.

Why is this important? Most, if not all of us, have heard about the butterfly effect (Lorenz, 1993). While I do not personally know if the butterfly effect is possible from a practical aspect, I do believe it could be true from a theoretical perspective. This would then support the framework that even our smallest experiences and decisions may have a significant impact on current and future events, experiences, and decisions.

For example, sometimes I find myself checking and responding to emails first thing in the morning. Call it excitement to start the day, enthusiasm for what I do, or simply passion for my career. This may appear to be a fairly mundane task or habit some of us partake in each and every day. However, what I find happening (when I do not make a conscious effort) is those few moments quickly slide into an hour or two. So what, right? That is okay if I have time in my schedule however, most days I do not plan for two hours of early morning emails. Normally, I only intentionally allocate about 30 minutes or so and focus only on important emails; I get to the rest later in the day. Otherwise, I may have to reprioritize the rest of my day around my compulsive 1.5-hour email reading mishap. This 1.5-hour loss of unplanned time will most certainly encroach on the rest of the day. So, when we think we are being transparent with ourselves, we need to ensure we are being consciously aware; not just transparent in the moment or between text messages and meetings. Something as small as reading a few extra emails (or several in my case), can have an impact later in the day.

Often, we find ourselves in a job that we do well. When that happens, we tend to find ourselves going into a sort of cruise control or auto pilot mode. We know what needs to be done in our job and when to do it, and how to do it well. The result is we tend to take for granted what it is that we do, and just go through the motions at work. Has anyone asked you what your job entails? Most of us have been asked that question, right? What was your answer? I would suspect it was a well-rehearsed high-level generalization about the overarching things you do. But what do you *really* do? I bet there is way more to your job than you briefly described. What about the subtle nuances and experiences you have learned over the years? Those experiences and lessons count too.

Not too long ago, I was helping a client with her resume by conducting an experiential extraction (more on this later). She had completed her master's degree the year prior and wanted to help with positioning her career for a lateral position to gain more industry experience. I asked her what she did for work, and she replied she was an entry level financial advisor for a small credit union. I learned she had worked a few other places before that in the same industry through casual conversation. During this critical phase, I learned she actually had 14 years of experience in the finance industry as an account manager. I also learned she was fluent (in all forms) in FIVE languages AND had six years of experience in international banking and finance. None of that showed up on her resume. It was not that she did not know she had it, she was just not self-aware. This explained why she was being passed over (without explanation) for lateral jobs that her manager had told her to apply for. Once she understood and became aware of what she really had to offer, it was easy for her to see she should be applying for much higher-level positions. She had spoken five languages her entire life and had immigrated to the U. S. several years prior. To her, speaking five languages fluently was normal. The country she had immigrated from seemed like a lifetime ago to her but in reality, it was not; it had only been a handful of years. She was so focused on trying to make a great life and career (and she had done a great job thus far), that she did not pay much attention to her past experiences and their associated value to her present career position.

## *Self-Honesty Transparency*

This is a direct extension of Self-awareness transparency. This applies to both over or under estimating your value and skills. Most of us know better than to over embellish about our skills, capabilities, and experiences. However, I still occasionally encounter boastful managers and leaders who, while their stories are good, cannot back up or support their stories with the skills and talent they claim to possess. More frequently however, I encounter people who under estimate their value and skills. It is my belief that this has less to do with them as people and more to do with how they have been managed and lead throughout their careers. Over time, and through much supervisory repetition, they have come to believe that their skill level is average or even slightly sub-par. Yet they tell me about their many accomplishments and many proud moments of recognition in their job and career.

Another of my clients came to me seeking career positioning assistance. He had completed his master's degree a couple years prior in accounting. He was concerned about not having full time work for nearly two years and was contemplating going back for a second master's degree, perhaps in another field. He stated he had held a few part time accounting jobs but nothing full time. When I asked what he wanted to do, he replied someday he would want to have his own business but for now he just wanted a job. When we conducted an Experiential Extraction, I learned he had 10 years of tax accounting experience that began right after he had completed his bachelor's degree. He also had "regular" part-time seasonal tax accounting jobs with half a dozen different businesses and several personal clients for the past ten years; a few of which were Certified Public Accountants (CPAs). In addition, he had an accounting business web site for when he was able to "have his own business".

We did a quick check on the state web site and learned he more than likely had accumulated enough experience to sit for the state CPA exam. What had transpired was that he was not honest with himself about his experience and value. He had accepted working for part-time wages for those other companies instead of charging them "his" rate for his accounting expertise. He had admitted many of his employers repeatedly told him he did not have enough full-time experience and therefore had been perceived to have low value. Yet, these were the same companies who repeatedly and consistently hired him to work special projects, or to help them to get caught up after other full-time employees did not work out. It appeared he definitely had the skills to perform. However, his employers had caused him to undervalue himself. The

Experiential Extraction helped him to recognize and understand his true value.

## *Planning Transparency*

Planning transparency pertains to the efficacy of our career planning. When we are developing or updating our personal and professional career plans, we sometimes may over or under evaluate the tasks and sub-goals that go into reaching those primary goals. Over planning can result in the incorporation of too much minutia. Under-planning can result in not enough detail or simply ignoring minor or major tasks to make the goal seem more quickly achievable or attainable. Both are recipes for frustration. If we include too much detail and minutia, we can become overwhelmed by the number of tasks. This can then lead to demotivation, and the whole process becomes a slippery slope with a negative trend. Conversely, failing to highlight tasks, and milestones sufficiently in our planning can over simplify our goal. This too will create self-doubt about the potential to achieve the goal or unrealistic goal performance expectations. What we need to do is to strike the right balance.

I recall when just starting my doctoral program, I had developed a plan for allocating my study time while working full-time and maintaining a healthy family environment balance. I remember developing this detailed spreadsheet with the hours I was going to do school work each day, and which study tasks I was going to accomplish on those days. I did this for an entire 12-week semester. Within the first month I was completely overwhelmed. I began doubting I would be able to finish the semester with a worthy grade, let alone be able sustain the plan to finish the program. I was tracking all my study activities. The more I tracked, the more I realized I was not sticking to my schedule. The more I saw that I was not sticking to my schedule the more frustrated I became (this is the slippery slope I mentioned). I reached out to a fellow colleague and realized I had incorporated too much detail and minutia in my planning – on the plus side, it was an EXTREMELY transparent and detailed plan. I determined I needed to "thin out" my plan. My revised plan included the days I had required activities to complete, and the start dates and due dates of my assignments. This worked MUCH better as it allowed me the flexibility to self-manage my learning schedule. Some days I would do a bit more work, some days a bit less. As long as my assignments were submitted on time, that was all that mattered. The lessons here were finding a balance about expectations and performance schedule, and accept a level of flexibility. These ultimately lead to better quality assignments and more manageable goals. While I used this experience during my doctoral program (educational planning) as an example, the thought process can be applied equally well to personal and professional planning.

# 9 - Types of Career Positioning

I have identified three primary types of career positioning: internal, predetermined, and unanticipated. Categorically, they are the three high level scenarios we should always be prepared for. When done properly, each type of career positioning should prepare you for each of these positioning scenarios. By deliberately focusing on each category during the planning phase, you can achieve specific targeted results. Let us explore these three types of career positioning further.

## *Internal Positioning*

Internal positioning involves positioning oneself for a promotion, lateral move, or a move due to an restructuring or reorganization. I have personally utilized internal positioning for each of these scenarios. In theory, we should always be looking towards, and planning for, internal positioning opportunities. This type of positioning facilitates career growth and advancement. And, it will most certainly increase your business and industry acumen.

*Promotion.*

In preparation for a promotion, I have always strived towards being considered a subject matter expert by others in the job area I was trying to promote into. Becoming a subject matter expert entails becoming a knowledge sponge whereby we are always asking questions, seeking answers, and conducting job related procedural research. It can also include pursuing academic credentialing in the form of additional degrees or certifications. When I was working as an operations policies and procedures administrator for a defense contractor, I became a subject matter expert on what meaningful policies and procedures should look like. I conducted industry research on how to benchmark against industry best practices in order to increase the effectiveness of policies and procedures. This enabled me to streamline our policies and procedures processes. As a result, I was rewarded with a promotion.

*Lateral.*

Continuing this story from a lateral positioning perspective, I was not only a subject matter expert in the operations department, I was considered extremely knowledgeable in areas of security, and environmental health and safety (EHS). At the time, the security and EHS departments fell under operations, yet were individually directed. I could have focused only on operations, but I did not – I focused on all three departments. Ultimately, this was to my own detriment. I reduced document cycle time by 30% and significantly increased the effectiveness of the policies and procedures. The results were so effective and efficient, I worked myself out of my job. How did that happen though? Well initially, my position was the result of having too many convoluted policies and procedures, and there was a need for someone to coordinate and manage the policies and related processes. Due to my expertise, I refined the policies and processes in such a way that each owning department could effectively manage their own policies and procedures through following and adhering to the refinements I had developed. From a departmental financial perspective, this was a good thing. It did leave me in a bit of a pickle though. The good news is, since I had internally positioned myself well, it opened up a lateral opportunity for me to gain additional experience through supporting several quality related projects involving Six Sigma and Lean improvement initiatives. This further extended my experience and credentials in a way that truly improved my internal positioning.

*Restructuring (Re-Organization).*

This same story continues into the next category of career positioning. After several months of providing Six Sigma and Lean project support, the company indicated there would be a major internal overhaul and reorganization. Since I had the least amount of departmental tenure, my name immediately floated to the top of the list for those to be impacted most by the reorganization efforts. Fortunately, due to my continued career positioning diligence, I was able to capitalize on my efforts. I began contacting my company peers and their managers, and letting them know about my upcoming availability. Within a few weeks, I was absorbed by another organization that found value in my property management and organizational efficiency experience.

## *Predetermined Positioning*

Predetermined positioning involves preparing for a known end result. You are effectively planning for a known predetermined future event. For example, it positions you for career alignment, voluntary quit or resignation scenarios, end of contract, or retirement. I have utilized predetermined positioning in each of these scenarios except retirement – I enjoy what I do too much to retire at this moment, but the same principles apply. In theory, we should always be planning for predetermined positioning opportunities as part of our backup plan. This type of positioning facilitates career opportunity awareness and can potentially lead to external career opportunities.

### *Career Alignment.*

Career alignment is the result of critical reflection and preparation. You may choose to pursue career alignment for several reasons. Perhaps you have experienced job burnout. Maybe you realized this was not the job you wanted. Maybe you are ready for a job or career change, perhaps something that better aligns with your education and/or experience. Or, maybe this is going to be a second or third career for you. For me, it was that I was ready for a change. I had been working for a defense contractor for eight and a half years, and had completed my doctorate the year prior. As a result, I wanted to pursue a role with increased responsibility.

My education and experience had positioned me well for opportunities outside the company, so I started applying to openings at other firms. Within a few months, I had attended several interviews, and was offered (and accepted) a job in program management with a large technology software company.

*Voluntary Quit/Resignation.*

Voluntary quit/resignation is also the result of critical reflection and preparation. You may choose to resign from a job for several reasons. Much like career alignment, perhaps you too have experienced job burn out. Perhaps you realized the job you have is not the job you wanted. Maybe, you realized you are ready for a job or career change. Or, maybe this is going to be a second or third career for you. For me, it was a combination of burn out and readiness for a change.

The first job I took after I completed my first tour in the military was a security role at a casino. I knew that job was only temporary because, at the time, I wanted to pursue a career in law enforcement – ideally as a civilian police officer. I ended up working for state corrections. I felt this would increase my business acumen and I could use corrections as a quick stepping stone into becoming a police officer. This "quick" stepping stone lasted five and a half years. During that time, I was promoted twice. Both times I was promoted as soon as I was eligible. My second promotion was to a shift supervisor/manager position – sergeant. While I loved managing and supervising staff (as I had in the military for several years), it came with a price – a 20% pay cut. During my time working at the prison, I had worked various unit security levels: medium, maximum, super-maximum, and violent sex offender.

The job took a toll on me personally and professionally. On a personal level, my parents, family, and friends all observed a marked difference in my personality. During the first two years, I had become cold, distant, hard, and a bit socially paranoid – gone was the fun and easy-going person they once knew. My marriage suffered, I divorced and remarried, and divorced again – each relationship was worse than the previous. Professionally, my record was spotless, and I was regarded as an exceptionally high performing officer and supervisor. However, there were negative cultural nuances I was not willing to accept. I could not see myself working in the prison system as my "forever" career.

The prison was an inherently hostile, negative, and, dare I say, evil environment. There were some good staff working there however, there were also some very bad employees. Additionally, I worked with the worst and most violent offenders in the state. I realized it was not where I wanted to be and made the choice resign. When I resigned from the prison, I had started attending college full time six months earlier, and had just joined the Air National Guard. This was my third enlistment in the military, and I was confident I could get full time orders within a few months. That was my backup plan. I had planned to not work for two months after I resigned from my position at the prison, and live off my savings. This was deliberate because I knew I needed some time to reflect and plan. I also needed to do some conscious work towards getting my mindset back into a good/positive place. Eventually, it would take me three years to become the Dave I was prior to starting work at the prison.

Everything fell into place just as I had planned. The time off was a much-needed mental vacation from the negative work environment of the prison. The full-time military orders also happened according to plan and two months after resigning from the prison, I was working full time in the Air National Guard in Security Forces.

*Term of Contract.*

Term of contract is working until the end of an established contract – a known end date. Term of contract can be in the form of temporary or contracted work, from project work (such as consulting), or the end of a military service obligation. I have experienced all three however, for the purposes of this example, I will refer to the end of my first term military contract, and my time as a temporary contractor.

While in high school, I had enlisted for a six-year term with the U.S. Air Force as a Security Specialist (Security Police; Security Forces). At my second base of assignment, as my contract was nearing its end, I had to make decision about whether or not to stay in the military. This was in the early 1990s and former President Clinton's administration had implemented a mandatory reduction in our military force. Due to my low time in and grade/rank, I was near the top of the list for involuntary separations. If I opted to stay in, I would have to promote to the next grade/rank as soon as possible. That would also mean I would have to score a 98% or better on both of my promotion exams. It was virtually unheard of for someone to score above the low 90%s. The average historical promotion scores were in the mid to upper 80%s. However, when a person scored a 98% or better on either or both exams, they were investigated for possible cheating and required to retake the exam(s). Since the involuntary separation lists were updated weekly, it would mean I would be living week-to-week until I promoted. Realizing this was not the most desirable way to live, I opted to get out of the military at the term of my contract. I had nearly three months of leave/time off saved up and used that time to look for work and adapt to civilian life. The key here is that I left on my terms, which allowed me to plan for the upcoming six months, and I was able to find a full-time job a few months after my military contract had ended.

Another time I utilized this positioning was when I worked as a college enrollment counselor. I worked as a college counselor, for a year and a half, soon after completion of my master's degree. Not wanting to remain in that role, I accepted a one-year contract as a property analyst working for the defense contractor described previously. During the first three months of the contract, I took copious notes and developed a nearly 100-page training manual for new property analyst employees. The result was a 30% decrease in new employee ramp up time. It also helped me establish a name for myself as an assertive and high performing employee. I was encouraged by my manager to apply for full-time positions within the company, so I did. At my three-month mark, I was offered a full-time job in the finance department. The defense contractor bought out the remaining time (9 months) on my contracted position so they could have me start as soon as possible. This was not working until the end of the contract in the traditional sense. However, it was from a performance perspective; whereby my performance helped influence an early buyout of my contract thereby expediting the end date.

*Retirement.*

While I have not yet retired, the principles for this type of positioning are similar to end of contract whereby a known end date is the target. Retirement does not necessarily equate to us not working. It just means we are no longer going to be working at that company as an employee in our current capacity. It is common for people to work after they retire. They may even work the same job but in a slightly different or reduced capacity. They could also work the same job but for a different company. Many companies now have talent retention programs with flexible arrangements for those willing to continue working past retirement age, but not on a traditional 9 a.m.-5 p.m. basis. Retirement could also be used to do something completely different. Additional considerations for this positioning may be future financials and income streams, target retirement funds, and anticipated medical, housing, and utilities expenses.

Ultimately, this will require mature financial planning and critical reflection to determine the retirement scenario that works for you. Specifically, whether you will be positioning yourself to work (part-time or full-time) or positioning to NOT work when in retirement. In either of these scenarios it is encouraged to seek professional financial advice. Additionally, it would be wise to have a secondary plan for an interim period just in case things do not go according to plan A or in the event you realize you miss working (it has been known to happen). You may be asking, what could go wrong with my plan to retire and not work? Some people retire only to realize a few weeks, months, or years later they still want to work. Having a secondary plan for retirement positioning means you would also be positioning for career alignment for re-entering the work force.

## *Unanticipated Positioning*

Unanticipated positioning involves positioning oneself for the unexpected, such as being laid off or let go. I have utilized unanticipated positioning in preparation for being laid off or let go. It is not a pleasant form of preparation to engage in – consider it planning for the worst and hoping/expecting the best. Many companies have a zero/no notice policy for lay-offs. This may be due to the company culture, or the perceived sensitive nature of work being conducted – in other words the company wants to protect itself from potential internal sabotage. However, when done properly, it is very proactive and can put time on your side.

### *Laid Off.*

No one wants to prepare for being laid off. Most of us would rather deal with this scenario when/if it happens. There is a fair chance that most of us will not experience being laid off in our careers. So why bring it up? Simple, to be prepared in event of this undesirable scenario. Remember, positioning is all about being proactive. Positioning yourself for being laid off will help ensure you have *active* options.

I recall when I worked for a defense contractor and had to prepare for being laid off. The company was doing well but had mentioned it was going to conduct an internal restructuring to increase departmental efficiency and better the company financials. We were also told the restructuring would primarily affect the engineering organization. Fortunately, I did not work in the engineering organization. However, what they failed to mention, initially, was there were going to be lay-offs (not just the simple internal department reorganizations). When the lay-offs came, it was a shock to many. Afterwards we were told there was only going to be that one lay-off round, and virtually everyone was at ease. At the time, I was with the company for just over four years. I felt relatively safe from any future lay-offs that may come but there was no guarantee. So, I took an active role and began checking my internal channels for other opportunities in other departments. I had several managers in my corner who indicated they would like to have me work for them. What I quickly learned was that my name *was* near the top of the list for the operations organization lay-off list because of my low departmental tenure – only two years. A short time later we would all learn that a series of *several* lay-offs would happen – without notice. I acted upon my positioning and accepted another job in the operations organization that needed my level of knowledge and expertise. Had I not been proactive about positioning for a lay-off scenario, I would have been in a much larger pool of people seeking internal jobs. Additionally, there was a very high probability I would have been directly impacted by one of the three additional rounds of lay-offs that ensued. In all, over a thousand people were laid-off over a six-month period. I was not one of them due to my proactive efforts in career positioning.

*"Let Go"/Employment Termination.*

This positioning is very similar to positioning for being laid-off. It too, is not a desirable thing to prepare for. Additionally, it requires a bit of attention to one's intuition, gut feel, and overall workplace awareness. I have seen very qualified professionals "let go" for the sake of benefitting company financials. I recall a close work colleague who was affected in this way. She was a mid-level salary employee who had been with the company for several years. She was considered an expert and was highly sought after by many high-profile departments and directors who depended upon her expertise in organizational effectiveness.

The company conducted a few internal departmental restructurings and required the department's 75 employees to "reapply" for their current roles. They were, in effect, internally applying to human resources to keep their jobs. This colleague was very qualified for her current role. She was also very qualified for several other roles at the same and higher levels for which she also applied. After a couple weeks, she was called into human resources office expecting to be told which job she was selected to fill. The news was not good. She was told to gather her personal belongings (i.e. purse/wallet, car keys, and clothing items such as a jacket or sweater), and that they/human resources would send her other personal work items to her via mail. They immediately escorted her off the property. She found out a short time later that lesser qualified employees had been selected for the positions she had applied for, and for significantly less pay than she was earning at the time. My colleague rebounded quickly and found other employment within a few months. Had she been a bit more proactive in her positioning, she could have sought outside employment opportunities several months earlier while still in the process of keeping her job. This would have gained her a few additional months in her job search, and potentially reduced the employment gap between jobs.

# 10 - Common Career Misconceptions

## _Laid-Off Misconception_

"This is a second chance, a do over…turn your dreams into reality."

I recall in the 1990s through the early 2000s when hearing someone had been laid off/let go, was just a polite alternative to firing them from a company. It was a kinder, gentler firing of sorts. While that still may be the case in some scenarios, there is a high probability that a person may just be laid off/let go due to a company's fiscal plan or a strategic response to market factors.

There are several reasons company leaders make a decision to institute lay-offs. Some are thoughtful and necessary, while others are short-sighted. Leaders facing significant disruption in their market may be forced to re-align their products and business models, which means adding new capabilities and experiences to their ranks. A lay-off may be the only way to accomplish this. Alternatively, strategy leaders may identify an untapped opportunity in the market that can become an engine of growth if they act fast and re-align talent. In cases like this, lay-offs can be a good way to thwart existential threats or expand into new markets. That said, getting caught in a lay-off is always unpleasant when you are the one unexpectedly out of a job.

There are situations however, when company managers impose layoffs as a knee-jerk reaction to market events like the housing crisis in 2008, or the ensuing recession. Such managers too often jump onto the cost-cutting band wagon, even when it has an adverse effect on their longer-term strategic position. In many cases, this is a result of compensation incentives being too heavily weighted on net profit rather than taking into account the wholistic health of the business. The result of such organizational tactics can be quite detrimental to the organizational culture, with the general employee population starting to feel like collateral damage. In many cases, companies likely do not need to take such aggressive measures. Rather, they have convinced themselves it is the best answer to a short-term problem. In fact, in many circumstances, it ends up costlier to the company to lay off employees than to retain them.

In cases like these, lay-offs were less about individual employees and more about short-term performance metrics that are no longer aligned with strategy. Highly qualified employees may be laid off to meet short-term fiscal goals even though there is evidence to suggest that it is more expensive to let go of existing employees than to train new hires. At the same time, critical skills and institutional knowledge may leave with departing employees. While it can often cost less to retain talented employees, tactically-focused managers can still tend to follow the antiquated and costly process of letting go and hiring new employees. The affected talented employees may begin to think they must have done something wrong – if this was truly the case, chances are the company would have pursued a formal termination (firing). Similarly, the recently laid-off employee may start to think they are not good enough or that there was something wrong with their performance – again, in many cases, this was not the case. If there really had been an individual performance issue, they would have been placed into a formal performance improvement process.

A company's fiscal plan may take various forms, and may include one or more re-organizations, restructures, or realignments. The company may also use various other soft or politically correct terms to convey the same intent. A company's choice to consider internal employee reorganizations may be due in part to it being bought out, cyclical financials, or simply a part of the company culture. In any of these scenarios, the company itself is not better off, except perhaps on paper or according to financials.

Some companies conduct scheduled *annual* employee reductions to remove "under performers". The misconception here is that the company's lowest performers may potentially be better than their competition's mid and top performers. When companies let go/lay off employees using a blanket percentage as a means of "fairness", they often hurt their company's culture and morale, and potentially their reputation. Employees want a company to succeed. When employees see businesses enforcing flat employee reductions across all departments, it essentially tells them that no one is "safe" in the company, no matter how well they perform or stack up against the total company population.

One common employee reduction technique is referred to as the "bottom 10%" (or "cream of the crop" or the "peanut butter" percentage technique). Whatever the name, the result is the same and it is perhaps one of the most damaging techniques of all. This technique stipulates the bottom 10% from each department is let go, or the top 10% is retained. The fallacy here is that one department could have all super star performers and another department may have a team that consists of primarily low performers, yet each will be affected "equally".

To help validate this view, I have observed several companies that have regularly used the peanut butter technique whereby all departments are required to decrease their staff by x%. This percent usually occurred in two to four waves of employee reductions, and usually affected from 5% to 20% of the staffing per reduction wave. The tragic downfall to this approach was seen during a 20% reduction, where department X's 10 employees were all top performers, and department Y's 10 best employees were lower performing than department X's poorest performers. However, each department was required to give up 20% of their staff – for the sake of fairness. The company lost two of its top performers from department X and retained eight poor performers from department Y. Instead, the company could have retained 10 top performers from department X and only six poor performers from department Y. To put the results in the form of percentages: retain 100% top performers and 60% poor performers OR retain 80% top performers and 80% poor performers, which makes more sense?

My guidance to you if you are ever laid off is to remain calm and embrace it. Use it as an opportunity to shine! Use this as an opportunity to: ask for, tactfully demand, or strategically negotiate better wages and benefits from your next employer. Take the opportunity to work for a better company or in a better position. Give yourself a well-deserved pay raise or a promotion by working for a different company. It may also be an opportunity to change careers or pursue an education or to finally follow your dreams! It all boils down to how you market yourself, and your confidence when you present yourself. Self-reflect and determine what you really want to do. Finally, be assertive in your decisions and efforts towards achieving your goals.

And, yes, ensure your status is accurately reflected on your professional media networks. You do not want to be accused of hiding your true status. As long as you have an explanation, you have nothing to worry about. The job market is stronger than ever, and companies are looking for highly qualified candidates.

I know this works because I have taken my own advice. I challenge you to alter your perception a little and create the reality you want. This is a second chance, a do over…turn your dreams into reality.

## Over Qualified Misconception

Many companies and human resources departments have a common practice of not hiring overqualified job candidates for a variety of reasons. If this is an internal posted position, this can lead to a decrease in organizational morale and frustrated employees. If it is an externally posted position, it can lead to missed opportunities – for the company. The bottom line is that we need to understand what is meant by *overqualified* and how we can truly benefit from these employees.

To many professionals, the word *overqualified* should not be an acceptable term used in a company's vocabulary. To overcome the invalid stigma of a person being *overqualified*, we need a better understanding about how a company really does benefit from hiring highly experienced candidates. I have assimilated four reasons why a company should hire "highly-qualified" candidates. The goal is to help provide you with tangible insights to overcome this misconception about a candidate being *overqualified*.

### The Misconception.

How many times have you heard about a person getting passed over for a job or promotion because they were "overqualified" for the position they had applied to? Maybe it has happened to you. How exactly does a person become "overqualified" for a position? I am extremely confident the term *overqualified* is never used when describing professional athletes, entertainers/movie stars, and university professors. I would also assert you will never hear a medical surgeon, or race car mechanic, or NASA space engineer being described as "overqualified". Can you just imagine how those conversations would go? "I am so sorry Dave, you are just too good a football player to play on our team" or "Dave, you are just too good a cardio-thoracic surgeon to perform heart surgeries at our hospital" or "Professor Peltz you just know too much about statistics to teach for our university". Why then is it considered acceptable in the business world and other working classes? How logical is this rationale in the workplace?

Since when is it a bad thing to have too much expertise, knowledge, and education? Our whole lives we are told to get more experience, get more education, get more knowledge. Apparently, some hiring managers think YOU CAN get too much knowledge, experience, and education. So much so, it will actually be detrimental to your career – look out professional athletes, surgeons, engineers, college professors, and movie stars, you may be out of a job soon! So, in other words, if I do not meet the minimum job requirements, I will not be considered for the job, but if I exceed the minimum job requirements, I also will not be considered for the job? Again, where is the logic and rationale in this thought process?

It is because of these idiosyncrasies we must explore the reasons for the misconception of overqualified candidates.

## *Reason 1-Misconception of "Overqualified"*

"You wished for $1,000 and won $1,000,000 – take it!"

I have read many posts online in professional networking sites regarding "overqualified" job applicants (internally and externally). I believe there is an inherent misconception regarding the "qualification" for a job position. Either a person is qualified (meets the minimum and/or desired requirements) or they are not. The question remaining is, if they are qualified, to *what degree* are they qualified? And, how do they compare with other available qualified candidates? Do they simply meet the *minimum* requirements? Do the meet the *desired* requirements? Or, do they *exceed* the requirements (*highly qualified*). Just because a person exceeds the job requirements does not mean they will be bored. On the contrary, they may bring additional insight, knowledge, perspective, and experience to the position and team. There is also potential that their high competence and confidence in the role will cause them to have a heightened sense of job satisfaction. For the hiring company, this may mean more "bang for the buck" for the employee they are hiring. Why would you not want to hire the MOST qualified person for the job if the candidate is willing to accept it?

We must ask ourselves, what is the *real* reason for not hiring the highly qualified employee? Is the company concerned the job offer will be rejected? Or, is the company concerned it is offering too little compensation for the posted requisition? Perhaps, they are just going through the motions and have already pre-selected who will get the job?

## *Reason 2-Candidate Application*

"It is the candidate's decision to apply to your company – be grateful."

HR recruiters and hiring managers repeatedly ask themselves: Why would a person who possesses experience that exceeds the minimum or desired job requirements apply to a given job? This is a valid question and ultimately one they should explore with the potential employee. I know if I was considering hiring a highly qualified candidate, I would want to understand this. Some of the answers might surprise you.

Answers may include that they:

- were laid off due to a force reduction or other similar reason;

Or, they could be:

- looking to increase pay and/or reduction in hours;
- ramping down in their career-preparing for retirement;
- looking for a second/their next career;
- retired but need/want an additional source of income;
- wanting to change careers/line of work.
- adapting to a medical condition;
- looking to reduce stress;
- seeking increased job satisfaction/gratification;
- aligning their experience and/or education;

- wanting more responsibility or less job responsibility;
- desiring a greater challenge;
- looking for a job that is easier;
- wanting to share and develop other employees;
- looking for ways to make a meaningful contribution to the company they work for;
- exploring a different industry;
- or, simply wanting a change in their current role (in life or profession) – it has been known to happen.

None of these are show stoppers. In fact, they all indicate the person still has a desire to work and succeed, and has a level of self-awareness that many of us should appreciate. Aside from the fact that it is a common industry stigma/practice to avoid hiring highly qualified job candidates, I would assert there probably are very few good reasons to avoid hiring a highly qualified candidate. One concern might be that this employee might leave after a short employment period. I would reply, ANY employee could leave after a short period of employment. So, what is the *real* reason not to consider/hire a person who exceeds the job requirements? I would argue there simply *is not* a good reason.

### *Reason 3-Fallacy of More*

"The hidden costs of many."

I have heard of situations when a hiring manager believes they could hire two less skilled people who meet the minimum job requirements for the price of one employee who exceeds the job requirements. The question then becomes: Is it really less expensive to hire two lesser skilled and/or lesser qualified employees versus one highly qualified employee? This could be true to a degree – at least superficially. When considering the total cost of this approach however, they could still end up with:

- twice the employee benefits,
- twice the employee trainings (hours and cost),
- twice the background checks/security clearances, and
- more than twice as long for experiential return on investment,

Given this, it is likely that this will not be a savings. Experience can be an exponential hiring consideration. There may be bit of industry propagated fallacy in the *real numbers* argument about two lower level employees costing less than one highly qualified candidate. It is quite possible the person with experience that exceeds the requirements may very well be more efficient in process, time, effective decision making, and overall performance; as they have perfected most/many of their skills. The math is rather simple, and the answer is: No, it is not more cost effective to hire two lesser qualified employees.

### Reason 4-Leadership Challenge

"Ensuring the right people are leading – it is more than just managing."

The real challenge, and question that should be asked here is, if we hire this highly qualified person, what are we going to do to ensure they are properly developed? This can be challenging because the person already retains many, most, all, more experience and skills than the position requires. This challenge ultimately resides with the employee's supervisor, manager, and leadership. The question to management and leadership is: What are you going to do to ensure this employee is properly developed? I would assert, a good manager, supervisor, and leader would create a solid plan to develop this person and work with the employee to successfully execute the plan. So, perhaps it is not a matter of should we hire a person who is highly qualified, rather perhaps the company should be asking: Does our management and leadership possess the necessary skills to develop a highly skilled employee?

## *Highly Qualified Wrap Up*

We now realize there are four challenges at hand for hiring managers considering highly qualified job applicants (1) identify who the manager wants to hire for the job, (2) understand the reasons why the applicant wants to work in the position, (3) consider the candidate's total true value, and (4) determine if management and leadership possess the necessary skills and knowledge to meet the development needs of the highly qualified employee. If we clearly understand these four facets (either as applicant or hiring authority) we can easily see there is limited justification for a hiring manager to pass up the opportunity to hire a highly qualified candidate. We should also realize, if a company does not want to hire a highly qualified candidate, the company probably does not have the requisite employee work environment and company culture to support highly qualified employees to achieve success. Ultimately, there is no such thing as being "overqualified"; either a person is qualified or they are not. If they are qualified, to what degree are they qualified becomes the point of differentiation. If a person has applied for a job, there is a reason for their application. The applicant should have an idea of what salary, wage, and compensation package they are willing to accept. Conversely, hiring entities should be conscious regarding the true benefits of bringing a highly qualified candidate onto their team. It may mean the company and/or hiring authority should adopt expectations of what it takes to become and remain successful in their industry. Hiring highly qualified candidates will set a high bar for individual and company performance expectations, and that should be a very good thing. **As a company, we need to ask: Do we want a company comprised of adequate employees or highly qualified employees? As employees, we need to ask: Do I want to work for a company who does not value me as a highly qualified employee?**

# Part III: Applying Career Positioning Considerations

# 11 - Career Positioning Considerations

This section addresses several career positioning considerations. It includes the four most common areas my clients ask about during sessions. Understanding and applying the information in these areas will:

- help guide reasonable expectations for higher education;
- help to assess appropriate salary/compensation;
- increase professional awareness through experience extraction; and
- facilitate positioning effectiveness by using positioning tips.

## *Higher Education Requirements*

I am a huge proponent of higher education. I cannot begin to stress enough the importance of completing a four-year college education. The potential personal and professional impacts can be significant. A college education will take you far in your professional career as long as you make this education work for you. The return on your education investment is well worth the effort. For me, a college education was a way to a better life, and to better position myself personally and professionally. Education often serves as a credential that opens doors. For some fields such credentials are imperative. In other fields, often it does not matter that much what degree you have or the field of study if you have the qualifications/experience required for a particular role. Below are some considerations for higher education and completing a college degree.

*Higher Education – Accreditation.*

There are several important factors to consider when selecting a college or university. Most importantly, ensure the college or university you attend is REGIONALLY ACCREDITED. A regionally accredited institution is held to higher learning standards. Conversely, a nationally accredited institution is held to lower learning standards. Furthermore, many/most regionally accredited learning institutions will not accept college credits earned from nationally accredited entities (with only very rare exception). Degrees earned from regionally accredited institutions are considered more favorable in the business world, and are the industry standard for virtually all jobs requiring a four-year college degree.

*Practicality of a College Degree.*

There are four primary degree types, these do not include certifications. The four primary degree types are: associate's, bachelor's (or undergraduate), master's (or graduate), and doctorate. Each degree requires a programmatic progression through their established course sequence. My college students and clients often ask about the "actual" need for having a college degree. My answer is simple and always the same – the more education, the better. Having a college degree will open up many more career opportunities. It will also increase your earning potential. The type of college degree and number of college degrees you have will help dictate the return on your education investment. The higher the degree, the greater the potential for an advantage in the workplace and your career. Having more than one degree at the same level (e.g., two bachelor's degrees, or two master's degrees) does offer some benefit. However, a question I always ask is: why complete multiple degrees at the same level when with approximately the same level of effort one could complete and possess the next higher degree. There are many potential answers to this question; some are personal and some are professional. I almost always take the position that it is better to attain the next higher degree, unless you are pursuing a specific field or curriculum that is prerequisite to the next level, or it is needed for the desired role. It is my belief and experience that a master's degree is better than two bachelor's degrees. The same would hold true at the graduate level: it would be better to have a doctorate than two master's degrees. To clarify into U.S. education level proportions, the following approximate percentages have remained fairly consistent since the early 2000s. Approximately:

- 38% of Americans have completed a bachelor's degree;

- 18% have completed a master's degree; and
- 4% have completed a doctorate degree.

Where do you want to position yourself from an education perspective? What type of education advantage do you want to have in your career?

*Additional Higher Education Considerations (modality, type, affiliation).*

This topic primarily provides further considerations that are based primarily upon personal preference. Additional considerations would be modality, institution type, and institution affiliation. Each is important and should be carefully considered.

There are three primary education modalities: traditional, online, and blended. The modality is more about convenience and cost to the student. The tuition for online courses is typically slightly higher than traditional classroom courses. However, there is much to be said about the schedule flexibility of online courses.

Institution type refers to its financial taxation structure. There are typically three institution types: non-profit, for profit, and not-for profit. In the early 2000s, for profit institution tuition was somewhat higher than non-profit and not-for profit institutions. Non-profit institutions include state universities and some privately held colleges and universities. Over the past five years or so, higher education has moved towards a tuition parity (with the exception of Ivy League entities). This tuition equilibrium has forced/influenced institutions to increase to the average cost of college tuition. You will still find some tuitions are a bit costlier and some a bit less than the average tuition cost, but most will fall somewhere in the middle range regardless of their type.

Institution affiliation pertains to whether the college or university is secular or religiously affiliated. My undergraduate and graduate degrees were from a for profit, private, secular university; and my doctorate degree is from a non-profit, private, religiously affiliated university. The inclusion of the religious perspective incorporated into the degree program provided additional insights into the education I received. Ultimately, these considerations are determined by you, the student.

# 12 - Salary and Compensation Expectations

There is often a direct correlation between education level and earnings potential. In most cases, the more education you possess, the greater the earnings potential. There are considerations that go along with salary and compensation expectations when positioning your career. Ideally, you should be competitively positioned with both your experience AND your education. If you are a recent college graduate with no real industry experience, the likelihood of entering into a job with a salary rate at the top of the pay grade is slim at best. Similarly, if you have 15 or 20 years of experience and no college degree, it is likely you will find limitations to your earning potential unless you have very unique skills and/or experience.

A good mix of college education and experience is preferable. If you have experience but do not have a college degree, then start school – now! It is better to say you have experience and are attending college working towards a degree than to say you only have the experience. Once you have a 4-year degree, it is unlikely that the timing of your degree completion will negatively affect the hiring managers decision.

*Salary Versus Compensation*

There is a distinct difference between salary and compensation when negotiating with a prospective employer. The difference can be very powerful and beneficial to you, if you understand your positioning and have done appropriate research. When done correctly, this positioning consideration can lead to great results. Ideally, you want to max out your salary and compensation package. Initially, salary and compensation should be negotiated separately; and then negotiated together to determine if you can secure a more favorable package. To do this, you need to have a very good idea what the salary range is for the position you are negotiating. Three good sources (I have found) for this are:

1. Glassdoor.com
2. Indeed.com
3. LinkedIn.com

These three web sites offer insights to salary ranges for a given company. You can also see local and national wage averages by industry and geographic locale.

I have successfully negotiated a very favorable total compensation package that was above and beyond the initial company offer. I will refer to this company as XYZ Inc. and had applied for a role as a Team Leader. I will also simplify and change the actual negotiated amounts. Prior to the negotiation phase with XYZ Inc., I had conducted research to determine what annual salary a Team Leader with my education and experience at this company should earn. I also researched the company web site to determine compensation benefits (such as paid time off, vacation days, sick days, insurances, company discounts, education benefits, etc.). The company started off all its employees with one week of paid time off. At my current job, I had four weeks paid time off with my employer at the time of applying to the other company. The salary range (hypothetically) for XYZ Inc. was $6k-$8k per year. That was significantly higher than I was used to earning but fair for the industry. I knew I wanted to start near the top of the salary range at around $8k per year. When it came time to negotiate salary, I was told the best they could do was $7k. I shared the research I had conducted and indicated it should be closer to $8k to start based upon the qualifications and experience I possessed. We then talked about how much paid time off I would receive. They indicated I would receive the standard one week. I replied that while the initial salary offer was a bit lower than expected, my bigger concern was low starting time off because I would be losing three weeks by working for them. The paid time off funding bucket is a different financial bucket than the annual salary funding bucket. The recruiter made a few phone calls and in the end they bumped my paid time off to three weeks! I again expressed concern that the pay was still lower than expected and I would be losing a week of time off. Then I inquired about sign on bonuses (this too is from a separate financial bucket within a company). The recruiter again made a few phone calls and stated they could offer me a one-time sign on bonus of $2k spread annually over a two-year period. This meant I would actually be making $8k per year for the first two years! I accepted the offer. I had effectively negotiated a package better than I currently had and better than was originally offered by XYZ Inc. But how?

The key was recognizing there is more than one component for the compensation package. Annual salary is one bucket, paid time off is another bucket, and sign on bonuses are still another bucket. In this case, I chose to accept a much higher annual salary with a slightly reduced paid time off. Another potential option I could have explored was perhaps accepting a slightly lower salary in exchange for even more paid time off. The latter is not uncommon in industry because, technically speaking, paid time off costs a company less than annual wages. That means it costs the company less to give you an extra week of paid time off than several thousand dollars per year in your annual salary. Additionally, sign on bonuses typically do not affect a departmental or organizational budget – they come out of a separate company level budget, and therefore should be negotiated last.

Understanding your total compensation position prior to negotiations has the potential to put you in control of your total compensation package. A caveat to this approach is being aware that government agencies and non-profits have significantly less room to negotiate in these areas than commercial enterprises. The most important factor here is to do your research – on the company, industry, and locale.

# 13 - Experiential Extraction for Resume Building

Not all resumes are created equal. Some resumes list a person's experience chronologically, starting with their most recent employer. Some resumes focus on a set of skills. Others try to blend the two. Most of the resumes I have seen and read are basically the same. They list the employer, dates of employment, job title, and occasionally a one or two sentence job description about each position held. The resumes I have read that are skill based simply list a few tactical job skills with brief descriptions of previous experiences. In both cases, I was left not knowing who the candidate was or what they had done throughout their career.

This is where experiential extraction plays a vital role in resume building. Your resume(s) (yes, you should have more than one type) are the tool that helps you get an interview. The interview is then your opportunity to sell/market yourself to the company to secure the job.

*Experiential Extraction Step 1 – Functional Extraction*

Experiential extraction starts with making a chronological list of your employers, job titles, essential job functions performed, start dates, end dates, categorizing essential job functions, and calculating the years and months of experience for each employer listed. This is most easily accomplished in a spreadsheet. This then provides the framework for you to identify your key experiential skills. This is also one of the most challenging exercises in experiential extraction. Clients become overwhelmed by either trying to list every facet of their jobs OR because they do not know where to start. Both are the result of being on autopilot in our jobs. This is not a bad thing, it is just a thing. We become so proficient at our jobs that we just do them. This is where critical reflection can help. Critical reflection can be used to "step back" from yourself and observe yourself from another person's perspective. One of the keys here is to look at and describe your professional self and jobs as you would to someone who knows nothing about what you do. This approach will help you to keep things simple and at a high level. It will take some practice, so be patient with yourself during this phase of the process.

### *Experiential Extraction Step 2 – Categorical Identification*

Once you have completed Step 1 for each job position listed, you are ready for Step 2 to look for repeating categorical job themes. Identifying those themes and the associated time in those positions will help you to create a list of industry skills. THIS IS A VERY CRITICAL TIME IN YOUR EXPERIENTIAL EXTRACTION DEVELOPMENT. It is at this point you will need to decide whether you want to continue pursuing and utilizing these skills OR position your career for something different. I state this because the skills you have been using may not be the skills you want to continue using or pursuing. If you decide to take another path, you will then take an active role in utilizing one of the Types of Career Positioning approaches from the previous section in this book. If you opt to continue pursuing your current position, you are now ready for the next step in the experiential extraction process – quantification.

### *Experiential Extraction Step 3 – Experiential Quantification*

While somewhat tedious, Step 3 is perhaps one of the most important steps in the process. It forces you quantify SIGNIFICANT RESULTS you have accomplished in your career within each job you have held. Using approximated or estimated numerical values is best here to help protect you from disclosing potentially protected company information. For each job you have held, you will offer a short description of your major responsibilities – this will vary by job and industry). Then you state the result(s) of your efforts. Next, you will want to quantify the facets of the description and results. These achievements can be quantified using dollars, percentages, head count, hours, percentages, increases or decreases, etc. The results help to demonstrate the value you created when you worked in those positions. It will also help to show and demonstrate the scope of your contributions and efforts. This can even afford you and opportunity to display you have exceeded the employer's expectations.

## *Experiential Extraction Step 4 – Final Build*

Your final additions to your resume should include your awards and accolades, speaking engagements, published works, body of knowledge, all college and formal education, and a one sentence hook at the beginning about what you offer to your prospective employer. Each of these sections will add to your resume to help your potential employer know who you are and what you will bring to their company.

When you have completed your final build, you will have what I refer to as a "detailed resume" (three to four pages long). You can then use your detailed resume to build a "professional resume". The professional resume extracts the information from your detailed resume to create a very concise high level resume (one to two pages) that is skill focused versus a positional focused.

# 14 - Tips for Successful Career Positioning

This section offers 11 reflective tips on how to successfully position your career. It serves as a reminder on where to keep your focus throughout the positioning process. Positioning your career will become more "fun" the more you actively engage in the positioning process. That being said, my definition of fun may be a slightly different than your definition of fun.

1. Getting started. This first step can be the most challenging – similar to ziplining or repelling down a mountain.

   The first step for just about any new task can be challenging. The first time you drove a car by yourself, the first time you jumped into the deep end of a pool, or the first time you moved into your first apartment or house. For me, it was repelling down an 80-foot cliff while in the military. I was never a huge fan of heights. But I took that first step and it was all downhill from there (literally). It was exhilarating to know I had conquered that fear that was holding me back. Many people are afraid to take the first step towards positioning their careers. Sometimes it is a fear of failure; sometimes it is not being able to see what the future holds; sometimes it is simply about change itself. As long as you have a plan, never give up, and embrace change as an opportunity for positive growth, the first step is just that…a step towards your future. Just like driving a car, the more you do it, the easier it becomes and the more confident you become.

Are you ready to take your first step…even if it may be a leap?

2. Take time to reflect often.

Self-reflection is a means to learn about yourself and solidify the knowledge you have gained. When positioning your career, it is an effective and useful tool to ensure you are maximizing your learning, and capitalizing upon your experiences. Reflect about key moments throughout your day while you are positioning. Gather data points from your interactions and positioning preparation.

What are the patterns that emerge? Are you learning from your experiences and applying what you have learned to better position your career?

3. Stay focused on what is motivating you.

Identify and take note of the things that motivate you. Are you internally or externally driven? Is it personal, professional, or a little of both? For me, initially, starting and attending college was externally driven. I wanted a better work environment and to earn a higher income. Working at the prison was not my idea of a dream job. Several years later when I started my doctorate degree, college was intrinsically driven. I wanted to learn for the love of learning and to be a good role model for my son. I found myself always trying to be the best at what I did for the love of always pushing my limits of learning…for the sake of learning itself.

What is motivating you?

4.  Take control of your career.

Admittedly, during the first few years of my military service I was not actively controlling my career. I did my job but drifted through the time wondering when would my career get better? To me, my career was something that just happened. I did what I was told, when I was told to do it. That was it. It was not until my supervisor encouraged me to take charge of my career that things started to change. I realized later at my second military station that my career was not something that happens to me but rather something I make happen and build. It was not an intangible object but rather something I could create.

Is your career controlling you or are you controlling your career?

5. Remember, very few things in life are worthy of stress.

   Many things in life that we experience are the result of frustration, not stress. Know the difference. Confront and overcome them with the appropriate perspective and approach. Sometimes, I have found myself thinking a situation was worse than it really was. I found myself dwelling on the issue… and the next thing I know the sky is falling, environmentalists told me that the oceans had dramatically receded, and lions and bears had mutated to the size of elephants. We have all experienced those moments. What is important is recognizing those times and putting them back into proper perspective.

   What things are you doing to ensure you are properly evaluating and approaching the situation?

6. Make a conscious choice to position your career.

   Do not take the approach to simply let your career happen to you. Rather make a conscious choice to take calculated and decisive actions to position your career. Like a college degree, you must make your career work for you. Completing your degree is a huge step forward, if you make it work for you. The same holds true for your career positioning. Being hired by a company is good however, you must make deliberate strategic decisions and choices regarding performance versus positioning to maximize your long-term career opportunities. Make your career happen on your terms. Choose when and how you will capitalize on your previous choices to project your career in the direction YOU want it to go.

When will you make a conscious choice to start positioning your career?

7. Remember career positioning has many different forms – be prepared for each.

Be prepared for all scenarios. While you may not need to utilize each of the different positioning types, you will at least have a plan. Some of your positioning plans may look very similar. The key is awareness of the various positioning possibilities. Being prepared for the various possible positioning outcomes and/or strategies will help keep you from being caught off guard. It will increase your control of possible career positioning destinations. Think of your preparation for the several positioning types as your own personal career insurance policies.

How are you preparing for the various career positioning outcomes?

8. There are only qualified or highly qualified candidates – which one are you?

Under qualified applicants will not be considered for a job position. So, when being considered for a job position, you are either qualified or highly qualified. The prospective employer may bring up that you appear to be overqualified, be prepared to have this discussion – tactfully and respectfully.

Many times, it is about perspective. When you show that you are actually highly qualified, rather than the misconceived overqualified, your true value becomes evident. Help your employer understand that being highly qualified is a very good thing for them. The caveat is you must first understand what makes you a qualified or a highly qualified candidate. You must also understand what your position is as a qualified or highly qualified candidate and what it means to you and your career.

So, which are you...qualified or highly qualified, and why?

9. A college degree is not an option – it is a requirement.

While there will always be exceptions in some lines of work (i.e. skilled labor and the trades), the value of college degree should never be underestimated. We do not live in a stagnate society. We live in a competitive and knowledge rich era. More information is available now to more people than ever before in history. We must have both experience and education to be competitive in the job market. A four-year degree from a regionally accredited institution has become the mainstream minimum for most jobs. It is never too late to start or complete your college degree. Every year there are many people in their 50s, 60s, and even 70s who are completing their degrees in higher education. Some people may argue they do not have the time, or they are single parents, or it costs too much, or...or...or... We can make excuses or reasons to justify anything we choose or decide to do or not to do in life. However, completing a college education should not even be up for consideration as a topic of debate…it is a requirement. View it as needing to have a driver's license to drive a vehicle.

What are you doing to complete your college education and/or your next degree or certification?

10. Know your worth and negotiate a worthy compensation package.

Once you understand your qualification level, you should then understand to what level you can negotiate your compensation package. You can gain this understanding by researching the company to gain perspective on the salary and compensation ranges for what you can reasonably propose during a negotiation. Compensation goes beyond just an hourly rate or salary level. You must also take into consideration paid time off, other company benefits, and bonuses the company offers. You must also remember that different forms of compensation can come from different buckets of funding.

What resources are you using to maximize your negotiating power?

11. Experiential extraction will differentiate your resume from others.

This is not your grandparents resume. Experiential extraction is about attention to detail, presentation, and knowing exactly what you have to offer. More so, it is about the quantifying your professional skills and experiences. You want your employer or prospective employer to know who YOU are and WHAT you have to offer them. You want them to understand that they need you because of your skills and experiences. Simply listing your previous employers, job titles, and dates of employment does not say anything about you aside from an obvious employment verification. You need to show them the SCOPE and IMPACT of your skills and experiences. Scope and impact is accomplished through quantification. Effective quantification demonstrates the scope/impact of your accomplishments and how this could apply to their business context and benefit them. Experiential extraction takes time and practice. However, just like your job, the more you do it, the better you become.

How are you capturing and quantifying your experiences?

# 15 - Final Closing Thoughts

As I have reflected upon my career so far, I came to the realization that it hinged on three key elements: transitioning (reactive), positioning (proactive), and conscious choice (deliberateness). How I have learned and adapted to new situations based upon my prior experiences helped me to make the necessary transitions from the military and effectively position my career. I also realized my career positions were not the result of luck or having friends in the right places. My friends may have played a small role in getting my resume in front of hiring managers, or letting me know when a job became available, perhaps even vouching for my performance. Ultimately though, it was my conscious choice to position my career that had the most significant and empowering impact upon my personal and professional journey.

Just as in our personal lives, we also find our daily groove and comfort zone in our professional lives. We set our alarms to get up a specific time, get ready for work, and get our children off to school. We travel to work, do our jobs, and return home to our families. The next day, we do it all over again until the weekend comes, and we take a brief break from our jobs. We are creatures of habit. Our daily comfort zone is our ability to master tasks and responsibilities. It is our life-long skills being perfected and tested every day. And, much of the time, we are on cruise control. It is just what we do – it is a rather reactionary existence, and it is okay. However, we should not take a reactionary approach to our careers. Our careers are not something that happens to us but rather something we create. We need to take a proactive approach; taking charge of our careers. We need to have professional career aspirations and goals. We need a strategy, and to have a plan to execute against. Our careers are vehicles to our professional futures. We need to make a conscious choice to steer our careers and not let our careers steer us.

Our careers are what we make them to be. They are moldable and malleable. Our careers can be adjusted and realigned. Our career aspirations and goals can change and be adapted to suit OUR professional interests, wants, and needs. Therefore, deliberate thought and planning need to be incorporated into understanding what we want our professional future to look like. We need to understand the variables and factors that comprise these elements so we can make educated and conscious choices to positively impact our careers. We need to have plans, and a backup plan, and a backup plan to our backup plan. We never know when our backup plan will become our primary plan. Our proactive approach and active positioning will help ensure our plans will be successfully executed and our career goals achieved.

We decide our careers, plan our careers, and guide our careers. We decide when to modify our plans, and the career path to follow. We are in the driver's seat. Take your career off cruise control, and drive!

With this, I conclude with one final career challenge question to ponder, explore, and reflect upon...

What are you consciously doing to take control of and position your career?

# About the Author

Dr. Dave Peltz, Founder and President of Peltz Consulting Services, is a leadership and adult learning subject-matter expert who provides career positioning coaching services for people in all lines of work and industries, including military and veterans. Dr. Peltz also teaches undergraduate and graduate studies in the areas of business, leadership, research, and statistics.

He attributes his knowledge, experience, and business acumen to three career phases: military and civilian law enforcement; corporate defense manufacturing; and leadership/business consulting. These three distinct and very different phases have provided him with broad insights on change and adapting to extreme or opposing environments. These experiences have enabled him to efficiently comprehend challenging situations and develop effective solutions through innovation and foresight.

Dr. Peltz has received numerous team and individual awards and recognitions throughout his career. He has also given numerous presentations, nationally and internationally, on leadership, human resource development, and adult learning.

He holds a Doctor of Philosophy (PhD) in Organizational Leadership with a major in Human Resource Development from Regent University; Master's in Business Administration (MBA) with a specialization in Global Management from the University of Phoenix; and a Bachelor's of Science degree with a major in Business Management from the University of Phoenix. He also has several industry-specific certifications and publications.

Email: peltzcs@outlook.com
Twitter: @drdavepeltz
Website: www.dpeltzphd.com
LinkedIn: www.linkedin.com/in/david-peltz-ph-d-84297b18

# Contact Information

Dr. Peltz offers a variety of services on Career Positioning topics contained in this text to include: seminars, presentations, workshops, trainings, coaching, and mentoring.

Please feel free to reach out to Dr. Peltz with any questions, comments, or stories you would like to share.

Dr. Peltz is best contacted via email at: peltzcs@outlook.com

# References

Bandura, A. (1969). Principles of Behavior Modification. New York, NY: Holt, Rinehart and Winston Inc.

Boone, C., de Brabander, B., & van Witteloostuijn, A. (1996). CEO Locus of Control and Small Firm Performance: An Integrative Framework and Empirical Test. Journal of Management Studies, 33(5), 667-699. Retrieved September 7, 2009, from Business Source Alumni Edition database.

Career. (2011). American Heritage® Dictionary of the English Language (5th ed.). Retrieved July 21, 2017 from http://www.thefreedictionary.com/career

Deci, E. L. (1975). Intrinsic Motivation. New York, NY: Plenum Press.

Deci, E. L., & Ryan, R. M. (1985). Intrinsic motivation and self-determination in human behavior. New York, NY: Plenum.

Deci, E. L., & Ryan, R. M. (Eds.). (2002). Handbook of self-determination research. Rochester, NY: University of Rochester Press.

Glassdoor. www.glassdoor.com/

Indeed. www.indeed.com/

Inspiration. (2016). American Heritage® Dictionary of the English Language (5th ed.). Retrieved July 21, 2017 from http://www.thefreedictionary.com/inspiration

Inspiration. (2014). Collins English Dictionary – Complete and Unabridged (12th ed.). Retrieved July 21, 2017 from http://www.thefreedictionary.com/inspiration

LinkedIn. www.linkedin.com/

Lorenz, E. N. (1993). Essence of Chaos. Seattle, WA: University of Washington Press.

Mezirow, J. (1991). Transformative Dimensions of Adult Learning. San Francisco, CA: Josey-Bass.

Mezirow, J., & Taylor, E. W. (2009). Transformative Learning in Practice: Insights from Community, Workplace, and Higher Education. San Francisco, CA: Josey-Bass.

Phares, E., & Lamiell, J. (1975). Internal-external control, interpersonal judgments of others in need, and attribution of responsibility. Journal of Personality, 43(1), 23-38. Retrieved September 7, 2009, doi:10.1111/1467-6494.ep8970064

Position. (2011). American Heritage® Dictionary of the English Language (5th ed.). Retrieved July 21, 2017 from http://www.thefreedictionary.com/position

Vroom, V. H. (1964). Work and Motivation. New York, NY: John Wiley & Sons Inc.